THE WONDERINGS OF

MARIGOLD HILL
PUBLISHING HOUSE

First published by Amazon in 2022

Printed in Great Britain

ISBN-979-8-83-864649-1

The editor has taken great care to provide accuracy of the poetry reproduced
within this book.

THE WONDERINGS OF WOMEN

Lucy T. Hill

To Marion and Terry Hill,
Who always encouraged me.

To All Women,
Never be afraid to express yourself.

To those that admire great women,
Always remind them of their brilliance.

C O N T E N T S

7 **MARGARET STEELE ANDERSON**

Allurement
Courage
Lost Youth
The Flame in the Wind
The Night-Watches
The Shepherd
The Trees
Whistler

17 **EMILY ELIZABETH DICKINSON**

A Book
A Day
A Snake
A Tempest
Asleep
Aspiration
Consecration
Desire
Forgotten
Immortality
Love
May-Flower
Melodies Unheard
Mother Nature
Vanished
Waiting

35 **MARIETTA HOLLEY**

A Song for Twilight
A Woman's Heart
Autumn Song of The
Swallow
Farewell
Aweary
Gone Before
Nightfall
Sleep
Summer

45 **FAY INCHFAWN**

Early Spring
In Somerset
Listening
The Flight of The Fairies
The Little House
The Witness

53 **FRANCES ANNE KEMBLE**

A Promise
A Spirit's Voice
An Invitation
An Invocation
The Wind
Woman's Love

CONTENTS

61   **EDNA ST. VINCENT MILLAY**

Afternoon On A Hill
Grown Up
Sonnets IV
The Dream
Wraith
Kin to Sorrow
The Little Ghost
Witch-Wife

71   **LOLA RIDGE**

Altitude
Art and Life
Dedication
Fuel
Iron Wine
The Destroyer
The Garden
The Fire
The Fog
Under-Song
Wind Rising In The Alleys

83   **SARA TEASDALE**

A Fantasy
After Death
A Minuet of Mozart's
Anadyomene
April
Barter
Broadway
Central Park At Dusk
Dew
In A Cuban Garden
Lessons
Riches
The Wanderer

MARGARET STEELE ANDERSON

1867 - 1921

Allurement

From yonder hedge, from yonder spray,
He calls me onward and away;
Broad lies the world and fair to see,
The cuckoo calls, is calling me!

I have not seen nor heard of Care,
Who used my very bed to share,
Since that first morn when, airily,
The cuckoo, calling, called to me!

My sweetheart's face? I have forgot;
My mother? But she calls me not;
From that green bank, from that dim lea,
The cuckoo calls, is calling me!

And I must go, I may not choose;
No gain there is, nor aught to lose;
And soon, ah, soon!, on some wild tree
The bird sits long and waits for me!

Courage

I thank thee, Life, that though I be
This poor and broken thing to see,
I still can look with pure delight
Upon thy rose, the red, the white.

And though so dark my own demesne,
My neighbor's fields so fair and green,
I thank thee that my soul and I
Can fare along that grass and sky.

Yet am I weak! Ere I be done.
Give me one spot that takes the sun!
Give me, ere I uncaring rest.
One rose, to wear it on my breast!

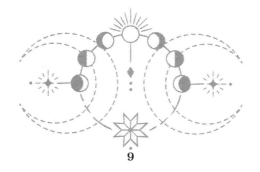

Lost Youth

He took the earth as earth had been his throne;
And beauty as the red rose for his eye;
"Give me the moon," he said, "for mine alone;
Or I will reach and pluck it from the sky!"

And thou, Life, dost mourn him, for the day
Has darkened since the gallant youngling went;
And smaller seems thy dwelling-place of clay
Since he has left that valley tenement.

But oh, perchance, beyond some utmost gate.
While at the gate thy stranger feet do stand.
He shall approach thee, beautiful, elate.
Crowned with his moon, the red rose in his hand!

The Flame in the Wind

Dost thou burn low and tremble, all but die?
And dost thou fear in darkness to be whirled?
Nay, flame, thou art mine immortality,
The wind is but the passing of the world!

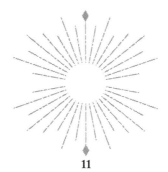

The Night-Watches

The laurel withers on your brow,
victor, weary of the race!
And you, who sit in mighty place,
How heavy is your scepter now!

Flushed with the kiss your lips have known,
"Woman, this is your hour to wake.
And know that flesh and heart may break
When love hath entered on its own.

And you, who knew where angels trod.
And marked the path for duller eyes.
In this lone hour are you still wise?
Do you not quail before your God?

God, to whom the dark is day.
Forget not these, the strong, the right.
The happy souls, for. Lord, at night
They tremble in their tents of clay!

The Shepherd

Thy slender form I think I see
On winter hills of Tuscany,
Thy slender pipe I think I hear,
So very faint, so very clear.

That lonely reed! It seems to me
To sing thine own simplicity,
For thou art but a child and young,
How should 'st thou know a subtler tongue?

Then, still a child, I pray thee pass!
I would not see thee with a lass.
Nor follow thee o'er grass and rock.
As thou dost lead some larger flock.

Ah no! That little, wilding pipe
I would not give for one more ripe;
E'en glad were I to hear it spent
Unchanged, and thou still innocent!

The Trees

When on the spring's enchanting blue
You trace your slender leaves and few,
Then do I wish myself re-born
To lands of hope, to lands of morn.

And when you wear your rich attire,
Your autumn garments, touched with fire,
I want again that ardent soul
That dared the race and dreamed the goal.

But, oh, when leafless, dark and high,
You rise against this winter sky,
I hear God's word: "Stand still and see
How fair is mine austerity!"

Whistler

So sharp the sword, so airy the defence!
As 'twere a play, or delicate pretence!
So fine and strange, so subtly poised, too
The egoist, that looks forever through!

That little spirit, air and grace and fire,
A-flutter at your frame, is your desire;
No, it is you, who never knew the net.
Exquisite, vain, whom we shall not forget!

EMILY ELIZABETH DICKINSON

1830 - 1886

A Book

He ate and drank the precious words,
His spirit grew robust;
He knew no more that he was poor,
Nor that his frame was dust.
He danced along the dingy days,
And this bequest of wings
Was but a book. What liberty
A loosened spirit brings!

A Day

I'll tell you how the sun rose, --
A ribbon at a time.
The steeples swam in amethyst,
The news like squirrels ran.

The hills untied their bonnets,
The bobolinks begun.
Then I said softly to myself,
"That must have been the sun!"

***

But how he set, I know not.
There seemed a purple stile
Which little yellow boys and girls
Were climbing all the while

Till when they reached the other side,
A dominie in gray
Put gently up the evening bars,
And led the flock away.

A Snake

Sweet is the swamp with its secrets,
Until we meet a snake;
'Tis then we sigh for houses,
And our departure take
At that enthralling gallop
That only childhood knows.
A snake is summer's treason,
And guile is where it goes.

A Tempest

An awful tempest mashed the air,
The clouds were gaunt and few;
A black, as of a spectre's cloak,
Hid heaven and earth from view.

The creatures chuckled on the roofs
And whistled in the air,
And shook their fists and gnashed their teeth.

And swung their frenzied hair.
The morning lit, the birds arose;
The monster's faded eyes
Turned slowly to his native coast,
And peace was Paradise!

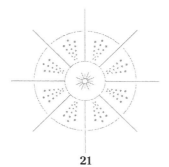

Asleep

As far from pity as complaint,
As cool to speech as stone,
As numb to revelation
As if my trade were bone.

As far from time as history,
As near yourself to-day
As children to the rainbow's scarf,
Or sunset's yellow play

To eyelids in the sepulchre.
How still the dancer lies,
While color's revelations break,
And blaze the butterflies!

Aspiration

We never know how high we are
Till we are called to rise;
And then, if we are true to plan,
Our statures touch the skies.

The heroism we recite
Would be a daily thing,
Did not ourselves the cubits warp
For fear to be a king.

Consecration

Proud of my broken heart since thou didst break it,
Proud of the pain I did not feel till thee,
Proud of my night since thou with moons dost slake it,
Not to partake thy passion, my humility.

Desire

Who never wanted, -- maddest joy
Remains to him unknown:
The banquet of abstemiousness
Surpasses that of wine.

Within its hope, though yet ungrasped
Desire's perfect goal,
No nearer, lest reality
Should disenthrall thy soul.

Forgotten

There is a word
Which bears a sword
Can pierce an armed man.
It hurls its barbed syllables,--
At once is mute again.
But where it fell
The saved will tell
On patriotic day,
Some epauletted brother
Gave his breath away.

Wherever runs the breathless sun,
Wherever roams the day,
There is its noiseless onset,
There is its victory!

Behold the keenest marksman!
The most accomplished shot!
Time's sublimest target
Is a soul 'forgot'!

Immortality

It is an honorable thought,
And makes one lift one's hat,
As one encountered gentlefolk
Upon a daily street,

That we've immortal place,
Though pyramids decay,
And kingdoms, like the orchard,
Flit russetly away.

Love

Love is anterior to life,
Posterior to death,
Initial of creation, and
The exponent of breath.

May-Flower

Pink, small, and punctual,
Aromatic, low,
Covert in April,
Candid in May,

Dear to the moss,
Known by the knoll,
Next to the robin
In every human soul.

Bold little beauty,
Bedecked with thee,
Nature forswears
Antiquity.

Melodies Unheard

Musicians wrestle everywhere:
All day, among the crowded air,
I hear the silver strife;
And -- waking long before the dawn --
Such transport breaks upon the town
I think it that "new life!"

It is not bird, it has no nest;
Nor band, in brass and scarlet dressed,
Nor tambourine, nor man;
It is not hymn from pulpit read, --
The morning stars the treble led
On time's first afternoon!

Some say it is the spheres at play!
Some say that bright majority
Of vanished dames and men!
Some think it service in the place
Where we, with late, celestial face,
Please God, shall ascertain!

Mother Nature

Nature, the gentlest mother,
Impatient of no child,
The feeblest or the waywardest, --
Her admonition mild

In forest and the hill
By traveller is heard,
Restraining rampant squirrel
Or too impetuous bird.

How fair her conversation,
A summer afternoon, --
Her household, her assembly;
And when the sun goes down

Her voice among the aisles
Incites the timid prayer
Of the minutest cricket,
The most unworthy flower.

When all the children sleep
She turns as long away
As will suffice to light her lamps;
Then, bending from the sky

With infinite affection
And infiniter care,
Her golden finger on her lip,
Wills silence everywhere.

Vanished

She died, -- this was the way she died;
And when her breath was done,
Took up her simple wardrobe
And started for the sun.

Her little figure at the gate
The angels must have spied,
Since I could never find her
Upon the mortal side.

Waiting

I sing to use the waiting,
My bonnet but to tie,
And shut the door unto my house;
No more to do have I,

Till, his best step approaching,
We journey to the day,
And tell each other how we sang
To keep the dark away.

MARIETTA HOLLEY

1836 - 1926

A Song for Twilight

Oh! the day was dark and dreary,
For clouds swept o'er the sun,
The burden of life seemed heavy,
And its warfare never done;
But I heard a voice at twilight,
It whispered in my ear,
"Oh, doubting heart, look upward,
Dear soul, be of good cheer.
Oh, weary heart, look upward,
Dear soul, be of good cheer."

And lo! on looking upward
The stars lit up the sky
Like the lights of an endless city,
A city set on high.
And my heart forgot its sorrow
These heavenly homes to see -
Sure in those many mansions
Is room for even me,
Sure in those many mansions,
Is room for thee and me.

A Woman's Heart

My heart sings like a bird to-night
That flies to its nest in the soft twilight,
And sings in its brooding bliss;
Ah! I so low, and he so high,
What could he find to love?   I cry,
Did ever love stoop so low as this?

As a miser jealously counts his gold,
I sit and dream of my wealth untold,
From the curious world apart;
Too sacred my joy for another eye,
I treasure it tenderly, silently,
And hide it away in my heart.

Dearer to me than the costliest crown
That ever on queenly forehead shone
Is the kiss he left on my brow;
Would I change his smile for a royal gem?
His love for a monarch's diadem?
Change it?   Ah, no, ah, no!

My heart sings like a bird to-night
That flies away to its nest of light
To brood o'er its living bliss;
Ah! I so low, and he so high,
What could he find to love?   I cry,
Did ever love stoop so low as this?

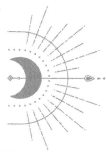

Autumn Song of the Swallow

The sky is dark and the air is full of snow,
I go to a warmer clime afar and away;
Though my heart is so tired I do not care for it now,
But here in my empty nest I cannot stay;
   Thus cried the swallow,
I go from the falling snow, oh, follow me - oh, follow.

One night my mate came home with a broken wing,
So he died; and my brood went long ago;
And I am alone, and I have no heart to sing,
With no one to hear my song, and I must go;
   Thus cried the swallow,
Away from dust and decay, oh, follow me - oh, follow.

But I think I will never find so warm and safe a nest,
As my home, in the pleasant days gone by, gone by,
I think I shall never fold my wings in such happy rest,
Never again - oh, never again till I die;
   Thus cried the swallow,
But I go from the falling snow, oh, follow me - oh, follow.

Farewell

Lift up your brown eyes, darling,
Not timidly and shy,
As in the fair, lost past, not thus
I'd have you meet my eye.
But grave, and calm, and earnest,
Thus bravely should we part,
Not sorrowfully, not lightly,
And so farewell, dear heart.

Yes, fare thee well, farewell,
Whate'er shall me betide
May gentlest angels comfort thee,
And peace with thee abide;
Our love was but a stormy love,
'Tis your will we should part -
So smile upon me once, darling,
And then farewell, dear heart.

But lay your hand once on my brow,
Set like a saintly crown,
It will shield me, it will help me
To hurl temptations down.
God give thee better love than mine -
Nay, dear, no tears must start,
See, I am quiet, thou must be,
And now farewell, dear heart.

Aweary

The clouds that vex the upper deep
Stay not the white sail of the moon;
And lips may moan, and hearts may weep,
The sad old earth goes rolling on.

O'er smiling vale, and sighing lake,
One shadow cold is overthrown;
And souls may faint, and hearts may break,
The sad old earth goes rolling on.

Gone Before

Smooth the hair;
Silken waves of sunny brown
Lay upon the white brow down,
Crowned with the blossoms rare;
Lilies on a golden stream,
Ne'er to float in summer air
Wreathed with meadow daisies fair.
Lay away the broken crown
And your broken dream,
With one shining tress of hair,
Nevermore to need your care.

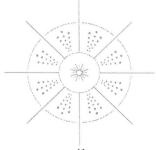

Nightfall

Soft o'er the meadow, and murmuring mere,
Falleth a shadow, near and more near;
Day like a white dove floats down the sky,
Cometh the night, love, darkness is nigh;
   So dies the happiest day.

Slow in thy dark eye riseth a tear,
Hear I thy sad sigh, Sorrow is near;
Hope smiling bright, love, dies on my breast,
As day like a white dove flies down the west;
   So dies the happiest day.

Sleep

Come to me soft-eyed sleep,
With your ermine sandalled feet;
Press the pain from my troubled brow
With your kisses cool and sweet;
Lull me with slumbrous song,
Song of your clime, the blest,
While on my heavy eyelids
Your dewy fingers rest.

Come with your native flowers,
Heartsease and lotus bloom,
Enwrap my weary senses
With the cloud of their perfume;
For the whispers of thought tire me,
Their constant, dull repeat,
Like low waves throbbing, sobbing,
With endless, endless beat.

Summer

Now sinks the Summer sun into the sea;
Sure never such a sunset shone as this,
That on its golden wing has borne such bliss;
   Dear Love to thee and me.

Ah, life was drear and lonely, missing thee,
Though what my loss I did not then divine;
But all is past - the sweet words, thou art mine,
   Make bliss for thee and me.

How swells the light breeze o'er the blossoming lea,
Sure never winds swept past so sweet and low,
No lonely, unblest future waiteth now;
   Dear Love for thee and me.

Look upward o'er the glowing
West, and see, Surely the star of evening never shone
With such a holy radiance - oh, my own,
   Heaven smiles on thee and me.

FAY INCHFAWN

1880 - 1978

Early Spring

Quick through the gates of Fairyland
The South Wind forced his way.
'Twas his to make the Earth forget
Her grief of yesterday.
"'Tis mine," cried he, "to bring her joy!"
And on his lightsome feet
In haste he slung the snowdrop bells,
Pushed past the Fairy sentinels,
And out with laughter sweet.

Clear flames of Crocus glimmered on
The shining way he went.
He whispered to the trees strange tales
Of wondrous sweet intent,
When, suddenly, his witching voice
With timbre rich and rare,
Rang through the woodlands till it cleft
Earth's silent solitudes, and left
A Dream of Roses there!

In Somerset

In Somerset they guide the plough
From early dawn till twilight now.
The good red earth smells sweeter yet,
Behind the plough, in Somerset.
The celandines round last year's mow
Blaze out . . . and with his old-time vow
The South Wind woos the Violet,
In Somerset.

Then, every brimming dyke and trough
Is laughing wide with ripples now,
And oh, 'tis easy to forget
That wintry winds can sigh and sough,
When thrushes chant on every bough
In Somerset!

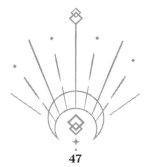

Listening

His step? Ah, no; 'tis but the rain
That hurtles on the window pane.
Let's draw the curtains close and sit
Beside the fire awhile and knit.
Two purl -- two plain. A well-shaped sock,
And warm. (I thought I heard a knock,
But 'twas the slam of Jones's door.)
Yes, good Scotch yarn is far before
The fleecy wools -- a different thing,
And best for wear. (Was that his ring?)
No. 'Tis the muffin man I see;
We'll have threepennyworth for tea.
Two plain -- two purl; that heel is neat.
(I hear his step far down the street.)
Two purl -- two plain. The sock can wait;
I'll make the tea. (He's at the gate!)

The Flight of The Fairies

There's a rustle in the woodlands, and a sighing in the breeze,
For the Little Folk are busy in the bushes and the trees;
They are packing up their treasures, every one with nimble hand,
Ready for the coming journey back to sunny Fairyland.

They have gathered up the jewels from their beds of mossy green,
With all the dewy diamonds that summer morns have seen;
The silver from the lichen and the powdered gold dust, too,
Where the buttercups have flourished and the dandelions grew.

They packed away the birdies' songs, then, lest we should be sad,
They left the Robin's carol out, to make the winter glad;
They packed the fragrance of the flowers, then, lest we should forget,
Out of the pearly scented box they dropped a Violet.

Then o'er a leafy carpet, by the silent woods they came,
Where the golden bracken lingered and the maples were aflame.
On the stream the starlight shimmered, o'er their wings the moonbeams shone,

Music filtered through the forest -- and the Little Folk were gone!

The Little House

One yestereve, in the waning light,
When the wind was still and the gloaming bright,
There came a breath from a far countrie,
And the ghost of a Little House called to me.

"Have you forgotten me?" "No!" I cried.
"Your hall was as narrow as this is wide,
Your roof was leaky, the rain came through
Till a ceiling fell, on my new frock too!

"In your parlour flooring a loose board hid,
And wore the carpet, you know it did!
Your kitchen was small, and the shelves were few,
While the fireplace smoked -- and you know it's true!"

The little ghost sighed: "Do you quite forget
My window boxes of mignonette?
And the sunny room where you used to sew
When a great hope came to you, long ago?

"Ah, me! How you used to watch the door
Where a latch-key turned on the stroke of four.
And you made the tea, and you poured it out
From an old brown pot with a broken spout

"Now, times have changed. And your footman waits
With the silver urn, and the fluted plates.
But the little blind Love with the wings, has flown,
Who used to sit by your warm hearth- stone."

The little ghost paused. Then "Away!" I said. "
Back to your place with the quiet dead.
Back to your place, lest my servants see,
That the ghost of a Little House calls to me."

The Witness

The Master of the Garden said;
"Who, now the Earth seems cold and dead,
Will by his fearless witnessing
Hold men's hearts for the tardy spring?"

"Not yet. I am but half awake,"
All drowsily the Primrose spake.
And fast the sleeping Daffodils
Had folded up their golden frills.

"Indeed," the frail Anemone
Said softly, "'tis too cold for me."
Wood Hyacinths, all deeply set,
Replied: "No ice has melted yet."

When suddenly, with smile so bright,
Up sprang a Winter Aconite,
And to the Master joyfully
She cried: "I will the witness be."

FRANCES ANNE KEMBLE

1809 - 1893

A Promise

By the pure spring, whose haunted waters flow
Through thy sequester'd dell unto the sea,
  At sunny noon, I will appear to thee:
    Not troubling the still fount with drops of woe,
As when I last took leave of it and thee,
But gazing up at thee with tranquil brow,
And eyes full of life's early happiness,
Of strength, of hope, of joy, and tenderness.
Beneath the shadowy tree, where thou and I
Were wont to sit, studying the harmony
Of gentle Shakspeare, and of Milton high,
At sunny noon I will be heard by thee;
Not sobbing forth each oft-repeated sound,
As when I last faultered them o'er to thee,
But uttering them in the air around,
With youth's clear laughing voice of melody.
On the wild shore of the eternal deep,
Where we have stray'd so oft, and stood so long
Watching the mighty waters conquering sweep,
And listening to their loud triumphant song,
At sunny noon, dearest! I'll be with thee:
Not as when last I linger'd on the strand,
Tracing our names on the inconstant sand;
But in each bright thing that around shall be:
My voice shall call thee from the ocean's breast,
Thou'lt see my hair in its bright, showery crest,
  In its dark, rocky depths, thou'lt see my eyes,
My form, shall be the light cloud in the skies,
  My spirit shall be with thee, warm and bright,
    And flood thee o'er with love, and life, and light.

A Spirit's Voice

It is the dawn! the rosy day awakes;
From her bright hair pale showers of dew she shakes,
And through the heavens her early pathway takes;
   Why art thou sleeping?

It is the noon! the sun looks laughing down
On hamlet still, on busy shore, and town,
On forest glade, and deep dark waters lone;
   Why art thou sleeping?

It is the sunset! daylight's crimson veil
Floats o'er the mountain tops, while twilight pale
Calls up her vaporous shrouds from every vale;
   Why art thou sleeping?

It is the night! o'er the moon's livid brow,
Like shadowy locks, the clouds their darkness throw,
All evil spirits wake to wander now;
   Why art thou sleeping?

An Invitation

Come where the white waves dance along the shore
Of some lone isle, lost in the unknown seas;
Whose golden sands by mortal foot before
Were never printed, - where the fragrant breeze,
That never swept o'er land or flood that man
Could call his own, th' unearthly breeze shall fan
Our mingled tresses with its odorous sighs;
Where the eternal heaven's blue, sunny eyes
Did ne'er look down on human shapes of earth,
Or aught of mortal mould and death-doomed birth:
Come there with me; and when we are alone
In that enchanted desert, where the tone
Of earthly voice, or language, yet did ne'er
With its strange music startle the still air,
When clasped in thy upholding arms I stand,
Upon that bright world's coral-cradled strand,
When I can hide my face upon thy breast,
While thy heart answers mine together pressed,
Then fold me closer, bend thy head above me,
Listen - and I will tell thee how I love thee.

An Invocation

Spirit, bright spirit! from thy narrow cell
  Answer me! answer me! oh, let me hear
  Thy voice, and know that thou indeed art near!
That from the bonds in which thou'rt forced to dwell
  Thou hast not broken free, thou art not fled,
  Thou hast not pined away, thou art not dead.
Speak to me through thy prison bars; my life
With all things round, is one eternal strife,
'Mid whose wild din I pause to hear thy voice;
  Speak to me, look on me, thou born of light!
That I may know thou'rt with me, and rejoice.
Shall not this weary warfare pass away?
Shall there not come a better, brighter day?
  Shall not thy chain and mine be broken quite,
    And thou to heaven spring,
    With thine immortal wing,
    And I, still following,
    With steps that do not tire,
    Reach my desire,
    And to thy worship bring Some worthy offering?
Oh! let but these dark days be once gone by,
  And thou, unwilling captive, that dost strain,
With tiptoe longing, vainly, towards the sky,
  O'er the whole kingdom of my life shalt reign.
But, while I'm doomed beneath the yoke to bow,
  Of sordid toiling in these caverns drear,
Oh, look upon me sometimes with thy brow
  Of shining brightness; sometimes let me hear
Thy blessed voice, singing the songs of Heaven,
Whence thou and I, together have been driven;
Give me assurance that thou still art nigh,
Lest I sink down beneath my load, and die!

The Wind

Night comes upon the earth; and fearfully
Arise the mighty winds, and sweep along
In the full chorus of their midnight song.
The waste of heavy clouds, that veil the sky,
Roll like a murky scroll before them driven,
And show faint glimpses of a darker heaven.
No ray is there of moon, or pale-eyed star,
Darkness is on the universe; save where
The western sky lies glimmering, faint and far,
With day's red embers dimly glowing there.
Hark! how the wind comes gathering in its course,
And sweeping onward, with resistless force,
Howls through the silent space of starless skies,
And on the breast of the swol'n ocean dies.
Oh, though art terrible, thou viewless power!
That rid'st destroying at the midnight hour!
We hear thy mighty pinion, but the eye
Knows nothing of thine awful majesty.
We see all mute creation bow before
Thy viewless wings, as thou careerest o'er
This rocking world; that in the boundless sky
Suspended, vibrates, as thou rushest by.
There is no terror in the lightning's glare,
That breaks its red track through the trackless air;
There is no terror in the voice that speaks
From out the clouds when the loud thunder breaks
Over the earth, like that which dwells in thee,
Thou unseen tenant of immensity.

Woman's Love

A maiden meek, with solemn, steadfast eyes,
Full of eternal constancy and faith,
And smiling lips, through whose soft portal sighs
Truth's holy voice, with ev'ry balmy breath;
So journeys she along life's crowded way,
Keeping her soul's sweet counsel from all sight;
Nor pomp, nor vanity, lead her astray,
Nor aught that men call dazzling, fair, or bright:
For pity, sometimes, doth she pause, and stay
Those whom she meeteth mourning, for her heart
Knows well in suffering how to bear its part.
Patiently lives she through each dreary day,
Looking with little hope unto the morrow;
And still she walketh hand in hand with sorrow.

EDNA ST. VINCENT MILLAY

1892 - 1950

Afternoon On A Hill

I will be the gladdest thing
   Under the sun!
I will touch a hundred flowers
   And not pick one.

I will look at cliffs and clouds
   With quiet eyes,
Watch the wind bow down the grass,
   And the grass rise.

And when lights begin to show
   Up from the town,
I will mark which must be mine,
   And then start down!

Grown Up

Was it for this I uttered prayers,
And sobbed and cursed and kicked the stairs,
That now, domestic as a plate,
I should retire at half-past eight?

Sonnets IV

Only until this cigarette is ended,
A little moment at the end of all,
While on the floor the quiet ashes fall,
And in the firelight to a lance extended,
Bizarrely with the jazzing music blended,
The broken shadow dances on the wall,
I will permit my memory to recall
The vision of you, by all my dreams attended.
And then adieu,--farewell!--the dream is done.
Yours is a face of which I can forget
The color and the features, every one,
The words not ever, and the smiles not yet;
But in your day this moment is the sun
Upon a hill, after the sun has set.

The Dream

Love, if I weep it will not matter,
   And if you laugh I shall not care;
Foolish am I to think about it,
   But it is good to feel you there.

Love, in my sleep I dreamed of waking,--
   White and awful the moonlight reached
Over the floor, and somewhere, somewhere,
   There was a shutter loose,--it screeched!

Swung in the wind,--and no wind blowing!--
   I was afraid, and turned to you,
Put out my hand to you for comfort,--
   And you were gone! Cold, cold as dew,

Under my hand the moonlight lay!
   Love, if you laugh I shall not care,
But if I weep it will not matter,--
   Ah, it is good to feel you there!

Wraith

"Thin Rain, whom are you haunting,
   That you haunt my door?"
--Surely it is not I she's wanting;
   Someone living here before--
"Nobody's in the house but me:
You may come in if you like and see."

Thin as thread, with exquisite fingers,--
   Have you seen her, any of you?--
Grey shawl, and leaning on the wind,
   And the garden showing through?

Glimmering eyes,--and silent, mostly,
   Sort of a whisper, sort of a purr,
Asking something, asking it over,
   If you get a sound from her.--

Ever see her, any of you?--
   Strangest thing I've ever known,--
Every night since I moved in,
   And I came to be alone.

"Thin Rain, hush with your knocking!
   You may not come in!
This is I that you hear rocking;
   Nobody's with me, nor has been!"

Curious, how she tried the window,--
   Odd, the way she tries the door,--
Wonder just what sort of people
   Could have had this house before . . .

Kin to Sorrow

Am I kin to Sorrow,
   That so oft
Falls the knocker of my door--
   Neither loud nor soft,
But as long accustomed,
   Under Sorrow's hand?
Marigolds around the step
   And rosemary stand,
And then comes Sorrow--
   And what does Sorrow care
For the rosemary
   Or the marigolds there?
Am I kin to Sorrow?
   Are we kin?
That so oft upon my door--
   Oh, come in!

The Little Ghost

I knew her for a little ghost
   That in my garden walked;
The wall is high--higher than most--
   And the green gate was locked.

And yet I did not think of that
   Till after she was gone--
I knew her by the broad white hat,
   All ruffled, she had on.

By the dear ruffles round her feet,
   By her small hands that hung
In their lace mitts, austere and sweet,
   Her gown's white folds among.

I watched to see if she would stay,
   What she would do--and oh!
She looked as if she liked the way
   I let my garden grow!

She bent above my favourite mint
   With conscious garden grace,
She smiled and smiled--there was no hint
   Of sadness in her face.

She held her gown on either side
   To let her slippers show,
And up the walk she went with pride,
   The way great ladies go.

And where the wall is built in new
   And is of ivy bare
She paused--then opened and passed through
   A gate that once was there.

Witch-Wife

She is neither pink nor pale,
 And she never will be all mine;
She learned her hands in a fairy-tale,
 And her mouth on a valentine.

She has more hair than she needs;
 In the sun 'tis a woe to me!
And her voice is a string of colored beads,
 Or steps leading into the sea.

She loves me all that she can,
 And her ways to my ways resign;
But she was not made for any man,
 And she never will be all mine.

LOLA RIDGE

1873 - 1941

Altitude

I wonder
how it would be here with you,
where the wind
that has shaken off its dust in low valleys
touches one cleanly,
as with a new-washed hand,
and pain
is as the remote hunger of droning things,
and anger
but a little silence
sinking into the great silence.

Art and Life

When Art goes bounding, lean,
Up hill-tops fired green
To pluck a rose for life.

Life like a broody hen
Cluck-clucks him back again.

But when Art, imbecile,
Sits old and chill
On sidings shaven clean,
And counts his clustering
Dead daisies on a string
With witless laughter....

Then like a new Jill
Toiling up a hill
Life scrambles after.

Dedication

I would be a torch unto your hand,
A lamp upon your forehead, Labor,
In the wild darkness before the Dawn
That I shall never see...

We shall advance together, my Beloved,
Awaiting the mighty ushering...
Together we shall make the last grand charge
And ride with gorgeous Death
With all her spangles on
And cymbals clashing...
And you shall rush on exultant as I fall -
Scattering a brief fire about your feet...

Let it be so...
Better - while life is quick
And every pain immense and joy supreme,
And all I have and am
Flames upward to the dream...
Than like a taper forgotten in the dawn,
Burning out the wick.

Fuel

What of the silence of the keys
And silvery hands?
The iron sings...
Though bows lie broken on the strings,
The fly-wheels turn eternally...

Bring fuel - drive the fires high...
Throw all this artist-lumber in
And foolish dreams of making things...
(Ten million men are called to die.)

As for the common men apart,
Who sweat to keep their common breath,
And have no hour for books or art -
What dreams have these to hide from death!

Iron Wine

The ore in the crucible is pungent, smelling like acrid wine,
It is dusky red, like the ebb of poppies,
And purple, like the blood of elderberries.
Surely it is a strong wine - juice distilled of the fierce iron.
I am drunk of its fumes.
I feel its fiery flux
Diffusing, permeating,
Working some strange alchemy...
So that I turn aside from the goodly board,
So that I look askance upon the common cup,
And from the mouths of crucibles
Suck forth the acrid sap.

The Destroyer

I am of the wind...
A wisp of the battering wind...

I trail my fingers along the Alps
And an avalanche falls in my wake...
I feel in my quivering length
When it buries the hamlet beneath...

I hurriedly sweep aside
The cities that clutter our path...
As we whirl about the circle of the globe...
As we tear at the pillars of the world...
Open to the wind,
The Destroyer!
The wind that is battering at your gates.

The Garden

Bountiful Givers,
I look along the years
And see the flowers you threw...
Anemones
And sprigs of gray
Sparse heather of the rocks,
Or a wild violet
Or daisy of a daisied field...
But each your best.

I might have worn them on my breast
To wilt in the long day...
I might have stemmed them in a narrow vase
And watched each petal sallowing...
I might have held them so - mechanically -
Till the wind winnowed all the leaves
And left upon my hands
A little smear of dust.

Instead
I hid them in the soft warm loam
Of a dim shadowed place...
Deep
In a still cool grotto,
Lit only by the memories of stars
And the wide and luminous eyes
Of dead poets
That love me and that I love...
Deep... deep...
Where none may see - not even ye who gave -
About my soul your garden beautiful.

The Fire

The old men of the world have made a fire
To warm their trembling hands.
They poke the young men in.
The young men burn like withes.
If one run a little way,

The old men are wrath.
They catch him and bind him and throw him again to the flames.
Green withes burn slow...
And the smoke of the young men's torment
Rises round and sheer as the trunk of a pillared oak,
And the darkness thereof spreads over the sky....

Green withes burn slow...
And the old men of the world sit round the fire
And rub their hands....
But the smoke of the young men's torment
Ascends up for ever and ever.

The Fog

Out of the lamp-bestarred and clouded dusk - Snaring, illuding, concealing,
Magically conjuring -
Turning to fairy-coaches
Beetle-backed limousines
Scampering under the great Arch -
Making a decoy of blue overalls
And mystery of a scarlet shawl -
Indolently -
Knowing no impediment of its sure advance - Descends the fog.

Under-Song

There is music in the strong
    Deep-throated bush,
Whisperings of song
    Heard in the leaves' hush -
Ballads of the trees
    In tongues unknown -
A reminiscent tone
    On minor keys...

Boughs swaying to and fro
    Though no winds pass...
Faint odors in the grass
    Where no flowers grow,
And flutterings of wings
    And faint first notes,
Once babbled on the boughs
    Of faded springs.

Is it music from the graves
    Of all things fair
Trembling on the staves
    Of spacious air -
Fluted by the winds
    Songs with no words -
Sonatas from the throats
    Of master birds?

One peering through the husk
    Of darkness thrown
May hear it in the dusk -
    That ancient tone,
Silvery as the light
    Of long dead stars
Yet falling through the night
    In trembling bars.

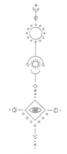

Wind Rising In The Alleys

Wind rising in the alleys
My spirit lifts in you like a banner streaming free of hot walls.
You are full of unspent dreams....
You are laden with beginnings....
There is hope in you... not sweet... acrid as blood in the mouth.
Come into my tossing dust
Scattering the peace of old deaths,
Wind rising in the alleys,
Carrying stuff of flame.

SARA TEASDALE

1884 - 1933

A Fantasy

Her voice is like clear water
That drips upon a stone
In forests far and silent
Where Quiet plays alone.

Her thoughts are like the lotus
Abloom by sacred streams
Beneath the temple arches
Where Quiet sits and dreams.

Her kisses are the roses
That glow while dusk is deep
In Persian garden closes
Where Quiet falls asleep.

After Death

Now while my lips are living
Their words must stay unsaid,
And will my soul remember
To speak when I am dead?

Yet if my soul remembered
You would not heed it, dear,
For now you must not listen,
And then you could not hear.

A Minuet of Mozart's

Across the dimly lighted room
The violin drew wefts of sound,
Airily they wove and wound
And glimmered gold against the gloom.

I watched the music turn to light,
But at the pausing of the bow,
The web was broken and the glow
Was drowned within the wave of night.

Anadyomene

The wide, bright temple of the world I found,
And entered from the dizzy infinite
That I might kneel and worship thee in it;
Leaving the singing stars their ceaseless round
Of silver music sound on orbed sound,
For measured spaces where the shrines are lit,
And men with wisdom or with little wit
Implore the gods that mercy may abound.
Ah, Aphrodite, was it not from thee
My summons came across the endless spaces?
Mother of Love, turn not thy face from me
Now that I seek for thee in human faces;
Answer my prayer or set my spirit free
Again to drift along the starry places.

April

The roofs are shining from the rain,
The sparrows twitter as they fly,
And with a windy April grace
The little clouds go by.

Yet the back-yards are bare and brown
With only one unchanging tree
I could not be so sure of spring
Save that it sings in me.

Barter

Life has loveliness to sell,
All beautiful and splendid things,
Blue waves whitened on a cliff,
Soaring fire that sways and sings,
And children's faces looking up
Holding wonder like a cup.

Life has loveliness to sell,
Music like a curve of gold,
Scent of pine trees in the rain,
Eyes that love you, arms that hold,
And for your spirit's still delight,
Holy thoughts that star the night.

Spend all you have for loveliness,
Buy it and never count the cost;
For one white singing hour of peace
Count many a year of strife well lost,
And for a breath of ecstasy
Give all you have been, or could be.

Broadway

This is the quiet hour; the theaters
Have gathered in their crowds, and steadily
The million lights blaze on for few to see,
Robbing the sky of stars that should be hers.
A woman waits with bag and shabby furs,
A somber man drifts by, and only we
Pass up the street unwearied, warm and free,
For over us the olden magic stirs.

Beneath the liquid splendor of the lights
We live a little ere the charm is spent;
This night is ours, of all the golden nights,
The pavement an enchanted palace floor,
And Youth the player on the viol, who sent
A strain of music through an open door.

Central Park At Dusk

Buildings above the leafless trees
Loom high as castles in a dream,

While one by one the lamps come out
To thread the twilight with a gleam.

There is no sign of leaf or bud,
A hush is over everything.

Silent as women wait for love,
The world is waiting for the spring.

Dew

As dew leaves the cobweb lightly
Threaded with stars,
Scattering jewels on the fence
And the pasture bars;
As dawn leaves the dry grass bright
And the tangled weeds
Bearing a rainbow gem
On each of their seeds;
So has your love, my lover,
Fresh as the dawn,
Made me a shining road
To travel on,
Set every common sight
Of tree or stone
Delicately alight
For me alone.

In A Cuban Garden

Hibiscus flowers are cups of fire,
(Love me, my lover, life will not stay)
The bright poinsettia shakes in the wind,
A scarlet leaf is blowing away.
A lizard lifts his head and listens
Kiss me before the noon goes by,
Here in the shade of the ceiba hide me
From the great black vulture circling the sky.

Lessons

Unless I learn to ask no help
From any other soul but mine,
To seek no strength in waving reeds
Nor shade beneath a straggling pine;
Unless I learn to look at Grief
Unshrinking from her tear-blind eyes,
And take from Pleasure fearlessly
Whatever gifts will make me wise
Unless I learn these things on earth,
Why was I ever given birth?

Riches

I have no riches but my thoughts,
Yet these are wealth enough for me;
My thoughts of you are golden coins
Stamped in the mint of memory;

And I must spend them all in song,
For thoughts, as well as gold, must be
Left on the hither side of death
To gain their immortality.

The Wanderer

I saw the sunset-colored sands,
The Nile like flowing fire between,
Where Rameses stares forth serene,
And Ammon's heavy temple stands.

I saw the rocks where long ago,
Above the sea that cries and breaks,
Swift Perseus with Medusa's snakes
Set free the maiden white like snow.

And many skies have covered me,
And many winds have blown me forth,
And I have loved the green, bright north,
And I have loved the cold, sweet sea.

But what to me are north and south,
And what the lure of many lands,
Since you have leaned to catch my hands
And lay a kiss upon my mouth.

Final Words

Thank you for purchasing this book of poems. It was carefully curated by the editor to include a variety of beautifully-spun poetry to excite the imagination, and to share the poems of women that are not always placed in the spotlight. It has been very important to the editor that the book felt relevant to modern audiences, and hopefully illustrates that poetry from the past can still be connective to contemporary readers.

If you write your own poetry, please continue to do so. It is so important not to lose sight of that creativity. Please share it. It's good medicine.

Printed in Great Britain
by Amazon

83410591R00056